Avalanches

STEVEN OTFINOSKI

Children's Press®
An Imprint of Scholastic Inc.

Content Consultant
William Barnart, PhD
Assistant Professor
Department of Earth and Environmental Sciences
University of Iowa
Iowa City, Iowa

Library of Congress Cataloging-in-Publication Data
Otfinoski, Steven, author.
 Avalanches / by Steven Otfinoski.
    pages cm. — (A true book)
  ISBN 978-0-531-22294-2 (library binding : alk. paper) — ISBN 978-0-531-22510-3 (pbk. : alk. paper)
1. Avalanches—Juvenile literature. I. Title. II. Series: True book.
 QC929.A8O84 2016
 551.57'848—dc23   2015031126

© 2016 Scholastic Inc.
All rights reserved. Published in 2016 by Children's Press, an imprint of Scholastic Inc.
Printed in China 62
SCHOLASTIC, CHILDREN'S PRESS, A TRUE BOOK™, and associated logos are trademarks and/or registered trademarks of Scholastic Inc.
1 2 3 4 5 6 7 8 9 10 R 25 24 23 22 21 20 19 18 17 16

Front cover: Skiers in Engelberg, Switzerland
Back cover: Rescuers search for avalanche victims in France

Find the Truth!

Everything you are about to read is true *except* for one of the sentences on this page.

Which one is **TRUE**?

T or F   All avalanches are triggered by human activity, such as loud noises, skiing, and snowmobiling.

T or F   There are three basic types of avalanches.

Find the answers in this book.

Contents

THE BIG TRUTH!

Working to Save Lives

3 When Disaster Struck

Researchers in the Alps study the snow to help forecast avalanches.

4 Rescue and Survival

5 Preventing Avalanches

A 2015 avalanche on Mount Everest was one of the mountain's deadliest.

Snowy days are common in ski towns like Andermatt.

CHAPTER 1

The Winter of Terror

It was an unusually snowy three days for the Swiss village of Andermatt in the Adula Alps. This popular ski resort was used to getting a lot of snow, but not 10 to 15 feet (3 to 4.6 meters) in such a short time. Then on the morning of January 31, 1951, it happened. A wall of snow tumbled down on the village. Avalanche!

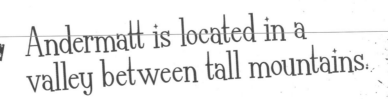

Andermatt is located in a valley between tall mountains.

Buried in Snow

The tumbling snow buried nine people in their homes. The villagers rushed to dig out the houses and rescue their neighbors trapped inside. But before they could do so, there was a rumble that sounded like thunder. Soon after, a second avalanche struck the village. It buried one of Andermatt's hotels, trapping the staff and five British tourists.

Some buildings were heavily damaged by the avalanche's powerful wave of snow.

Rescuers work to dig out avalanche victims in Andermatt.

Switzerland has more avalanche deaths yearly than any other nation.

Avalanche After Avalanche

The disaster didn't end there. Within the hour, four more avalanches fell on the village. By nightfall, the residents managed to rescue just two of the people buried in their houses. The final death toll was 13. Hundreds of skiers were left stranded in the village as snow blocked roads and railway lines.

The 1951 avalanches were devastating to the people of the Alps.

Alpine Disasters

Andermatt was just one of many villages and towns throughout the Alpine region to be struck by avalanches in the winter of 1950–1951. In the Swiss state of Valois, 92 people and 500 cattle were killed, and 900 buildings were destroyed. At Trins, Austria, an avalanche swept away an inn, a café, and a sawmill. In Italy's Zebrù Valley, 30 workers at a power project were buried alive in the wooden hut they slept in.

A Winter to Remember

Over a three-month period, 649 avalanches struck the region, taking the lives of at least 265 people. It became known as the Winter of Terror. To this day, avalanches continue to spread terror, destruction, and death. This is true not only in the Alps, but also in many other parts of the world.

Rescuers tend to a man injured by a 2015 avalanche in Nepal.

It is extremely difficult to get out of the way when a large avalanche begins.

CHAPTER 2

White Death

There is nothing feared more by skiers and mountain climbers in snowy areas than an avalanche. It comes swiftly, usually without warning. One moment, the snowy mountainside is still. The next, a wall of snow is rushing down the slope with frightening speed. You can't outrun it or out-ski it. Even a snowmobile isn't fast enough to escape what many call the White Death.

 If avalanche victims aren't rescued within 15 minutes, their chances of survival are slim.

What Is an Avalanche?

An avalanche is a mass of unstable snow that slides down a mountain slope. Avalanches don't happen on their own. Something has to trigger them. This could be a sudden rise in temperature, heavy snowfall or rain, strong winds, or even an earthquake or volcanic eruption. Human activity can also trigger an avalanche. An explosion or gunshot can start one. So can the weight of someone skiing down a slope or speeding by in a snowmobile.

Skiers can start avalanches by loosening snow on a mountainside.

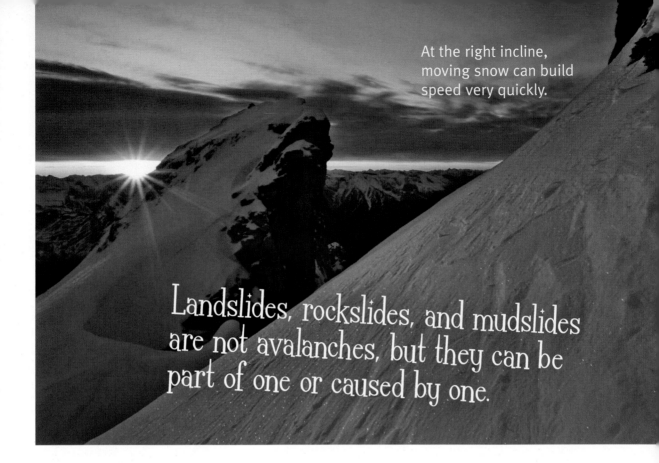

At the right incline, moving snow can build speed very quickly.

Landslides, rockslides, and mudslides are not avalanches, but they can be part of one or caused by one.

The Right Slope

Not every slope can produce an avalanche. If the slope is too flat, the snow won't slide down it. If the slope is too steep, not enough snow can settle and build up on it to form an avalanche. As a result, avalanches occur on mountain slopes that have an **incline** between 20 and 50 degrees.

The powdery snow of a wind avalanche can look like smoke or steam.

Wind Avalanches

There are three basic kinds of avalanches. A wind avalanche is made up of dry, powdery snow. It is lifted up by strong winds and falls down a slope at speeds of 200 miles per hour (322 kilometers per hour) or more. People caught in a wind avalanche feel the blast of air before the snow hits them. This kind of avalanche is often the least dangerous.

Slab and Ice Avalanches

In a slab avalanche, a heavy layer of snow builds on top of a weaker layer. The top layer eventually breaks off in a huge slab. As it slides, the slab can break up into smaller chunks. A slab avalanche moves much slower than a wind avalanche, but it can be far deadlier. In an ice avalanche, a large piece of ice breaks off from a mountaintop, often from a **glacier**. This type of avalanche is rare.

Slabs of snow and ice can be extremely heavy.

Slab and ice avalanches pick up trees, rocks, dirt, and mud as they move, causing much destruction.

Where Avalanches Happen

Avalanches can happen almost anywhere there are snowy mountains. Avalanches are quite common in the Rocky Mountain states of Colorado and Utah. Alaska has frequent avalanches as well. However, the largest number of avalanches occur in the Alps, a mountain chain that extends into France, Italy, Austria, and Switzerland. Also, there are more

avalanche deaths in Europe because the populations are greater in the mountain areas of Europe than the United States.

The Rocky Mountains are among the most common sites of avalanches in the United States.

Most avalanche victims in the United States are snowmobilers.

Snowmobiling in wilderness areas can be extremely dangerous.

Dangerous Backcountry

Ski resorts and ski trails experience few avalanches. Trails are usually well-kept, and the areas around them are monitored for any potential avalanches. Most avalanches occur in the backcountry, where there are few maintained trails and the mountains have unstable **snowpacks**. People who ski, snowboard, and snowmobile in these wilderness areas are risking their lives. Of all the people who die in avalanches, 75 percent of them are killed in the backcountry.

Working to Save Lives

The Swiss Federal Institute for Snow and Avalanche Research is devoted to the study of avalanches in the Swiss Alps. During the winter, it issues an avalanche warning bulletin twice a day for skiers and hikers. The bulletin pinpoints areas where avalanches may happen. Predicting avalanches is difficult, but there are some ways to figure out where they are most likely to occur. The institute makes its predictions by looking at areas where the snow is unstable because of weather conditions or because avalanches have occurred there in the past.

The institute's scientists analyze, evaluate, and research avalanches when they happen. This

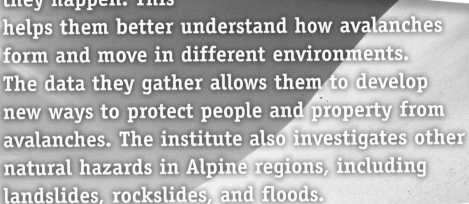

helps them better understand how avalanches form and move in different environments. The data they gather allows them to develop new ways to protect people and property from avalanches. The institute also investigates other natural hazards in Alpine regions, including landslides, rockslides, and floods.

Avalanches have been a source of disaster throughout history.

CHAPTER 3

When Disaster Struck

Every year, there are countless avalanches across the globe. Most of them take place in remote areas where there are few people. They cause few problems, if any. But those avalanches that occur where people, animals, and property are present are often devastating. Since ancient times, avalanches have taken many thousands of lives and destroyed millions of dollars in property.

A large avalanche can weigh up to a million tons!

Vibrations from an elephant's footsteps are powerful enough to dislodge snow from a mountainside.

Death in the Alps

The first recorded major avalanche disaster took place in 218 BCE. Carthage, a city in northern Africa, was at war with Rome. A Carthaginian army marched north through Spain with 90,000 soldiers, 12,000 horses, and 36 elephants. To reach Rome, they crossed the Alps. Coming down the steep mountains, the elephants' heavy footsteps set off avalanches. Before the army reached safety, 18,000 men, 2,000 horses, and several elephants were killed.

Afghanistan's Deadliest Pass

Another place famous for avalanches is Salang Pass in Afghanistan. The road through this mountain pass is one of the highest in the world. A series of deadly avalanches took place there between 1993 and 2002. Then, on February 9, 2010, a freak snowstorm set off a series of 36 avalanches that buried the tunnel running through the pass. Thousands of motorists were trapped in the tunnel. By the time rescuers could dig the tunnel out, 175 people had died.

Afghan rescue workers attempt to dig out victims of the 2010 avalanches.

Trains in Trouble

One of the worst avalanches in U.S. history took place in Wellington, Washington, in 1910. Two trains became stuck in heavy snow at Stevens Pass, north of Seattle, in February. For several days, workers tried to clear the tracks so the trains could move. Then a blizzard hit the area and turned into a heavy rainstorm.

The train tracks in Stevens Pass were built along the side of a mountain.

Workers stand among the wreckage of the trains in Stevens Pass.

On March 1, a little past midnight, a slab of snow 1.5 miles (2.4 km) long broke off a nearby mountain and came hurtling down on the trains. Both trains rolled 1,000 feet (305 meters) and fell into a ravine. The trains were buried under 40 feet (12 m) of snow and **debris**. It took rescue workers six hours to reach them. A total of 96 people died. Bodies were still being found three months later.

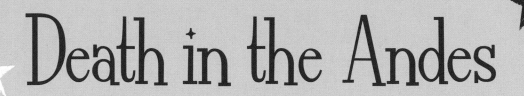

Death in the Andes

Ice avalanches are rare, but they can be deadly. On January 10, 1962, an enormous chunk of ice broke off from the top of Mount Huascarán in the Andes Mountains of Peru (pictured). It crushed seven villages below, killing at least 4,000 people. Eight years later, Huascarán was the site of a second tragedy when an earthquake loosened another ice chunk. Moving at 200 miles per hour (322 kph), the ice blasted through the ski resort of Yungay. Of the 25,000 people in the town, only 92 survived the avalanche.

These images show St. Gervais before and after the avalanche.

The Summer Avalanche

Avalanches occur year-round in some of the world's snowiest regions. On July 12, 1892, tourists and residents in the village of St. Gervais, Switzerland, were enjoying the summer hot springs. They were not thinking of snow at all. Then a glacier broke off the side of Mont Blanc, the highest peak in the Alps. It swept through the village, and some 175 people died.

If found early enough, avalanche victims have a high chance of survival.

Rescue and Survival

The statistics for surviving an avalanche are grim. If rescued within 15 minutes, an avalanche victim has a 92 percent chance of survival. By 35 minutes, that percentage drops to 30 percent. It is often impossible for victims to dig themselves out of the snow. In addition, it is a daunting challenge for rescuers to find buried people. However, there are ways to improve your chances of survival if you are caught in an avalanche.

Once the snow from an avalanche settles, it can be as heavy as wet cement.

A person must move fast to get out of the way of an avalanche.

How to Survive

The best way to survive an avalanche is to get out of its way. If an avalanche is coming toward you, quickly move to the side, out of the path of the fastest-moving snow. Grab on to a rock or tree and hang on. You will remain in one place and be better able to orient yourself once the snow has settled.

Create Breathing Room

Two-thirds of all avalanche victims die of **asphyxiation**. They are unable to breathe under the heavy snow. If you're buried, immediately cup your hands in front of your face to create a pocket for breathing. This could provide you with air for up to a half hour. Then move your arms out and try to "swim" your way to the surface. Try to poke your arms up above the snow so rescuers can see you.

In minor avalanches, many people are buried under only 2 feet (61 centimeters) of snow.

Once rescuers locate someone who is buried, they start digging right away.

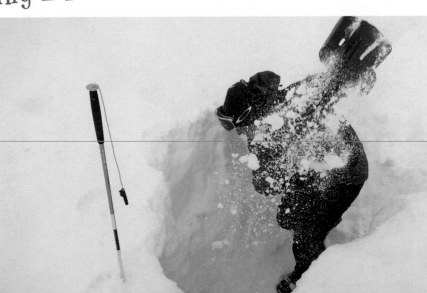

Avalungs and Beacons

Prepared skiers and climbers carry two pieces of equipment that will help them survive an avalanche. The avalung is a long hose that allows a person to breathe clean air from the snow. A **beacon** is a radio transmitter that sends out signals. Rescuers with beacons can pick up the signal and precisely locate an avalanche victim under the snow.

Rescue dogs are often used to find buried people.

To the Rescue

Rescue teams use equipment and dogs to save avalanche victims. Workers use long poles called **probes** to poke through the deep snow to find people. They also use shovels to dig them out quickly. Rescue dogs use their powerful noses to sniff out people hidden under the snow. When victims are found, they often need immediate medical attention. Rescuers use helicopters to transport them quickly to hospitals.

Alex White was extremely lucky to survive after being buried by a backcountry avalanche.

Lost in the Rockies

One of the most remarkable avalanche survival stories took place on March 2, 2013. Alex White, a 24-year-old law student, was skiing in the backcountry of northern Colorado with a friend. Suddenly, White saw "a cloud of barreling snow" coming toward him. The flood of snow pushed him several hundred feet. He was buried in it, and one of his legs was badly twisted.

At first, White struggled to get out of the snow. Then he realized he needed to conserve his energy. Fortunately, two other skiers had seen the avalanche and called for help. Rescuers dug into the snow with shovels. Then one man heard a groan. They dug wildly until they reached White. He had been under the snow for three hours. The survival rate at that point was just 1 percent! Amazingly, White was back in school within a week.

Rescue workers Sam McCloskey (left) and Andrew Maddox saved White's life.

Protective barriers on the side of a mountain can slow avalanches before they reach villages and towns below.

Preventing Avalanches

For many years, scientists and people living in avalanche-prone regions have been seeking ways to lessen the impact of these incredible natural events. For example, authorities sometimes use explosives to trigger avalanches on purpose. This allows them to direct the snow and ice along a path where they won't do much damage. These efforts are saving lives and property in many areas affected by avalanches.

Avalanche barriers can be made of materials such as wood, metal, or concrete.

Natural Barriers

Trees on mountainsides play an important role in slowing down avalanches and reducing their power. Unfortunately, over many centuries, forests in some places, especially the Alps, have been cut down for lumber and fuel. Growing new trees takes a long time. But effective reforestation programs in Alpine countries are helping to replenish trees in the mountains.

Timeline of Avalanches

218 BCE
Avalanches take the lives of thousands of soldiers crossing the Alps to attack Rome.

July 12, 1892
Some 175 people in the village of St. Gervais, Switzerland, are killed by an ice avalanche on Mont Blanc.

Human-Made Barriers

In addition to relying on trees to slow down avalanches, people have built giant mounds of dirt and rocks at the bottom of slopes. More modern structures have been built with wedge shapes to split sliding snow and ice to further weaken their power. In other cases, residents have filled their backyards with soil and rock to make them level with roofs. When an avalanche comes, the snow slides harmlessly over the rooftops.

May 31, 1970

An earthquake triggers an avalanche that wipes out Yungay, Peru, killing nearly the entire population of the town.

March 1, 1910

Two trains are hurled into a ravine in Wellington, Washington, by a massive avalanche, killing 96 passengers and crew members.

April 25, 2015

An earthquake in Nepal causes an avalanche on Mount Everest that kills about 20 climbers and injures many others.

Avalanches can give beautiful plants a new place to grow.

The Positive Side

Avalanches are destructive, but good things can sometimes come out of that destruction. When an avalanche clears out a section of trees on a mountainside, it may open up space for new life to grow. Where a forest once stood, a field or meadow can form, bringing a diverse mix of new plants and animals to the region.

A run-out zone is the area where an avalanche stops and the snow and ice settle down. The snow may contain nutrients from the mountainside that can feed plant life. When the snow melts, the water feeds and promotes new plant growth. The rocks and debris carried along by the avalanche can aid water drainage and help shape new routes for rivers and streams. Though avalanches can be dangerous, they are also an important part of nature. ★

A new mountain stream can be formed as the result of an avalanche.

Number of avalanches that occur in the western United States each year: 100,000

Average number of people killed worldwide by avalanches each year: 122

Countries with the highest risk of avalanches: Austria, Switzerland, Italy, France, and the United States

States with the most avalanches: Alaska, Colorado, and Utah

Percentage of avalanche victims in backcountry and extreme wilderness areas: 75 percent

Average worldwide economic damage from avalanches each year: $27,844,000

Did you find the truth?

All avalanches are triggered by human activity, such as loud noises, skiing, and snowmobiling.

There are three basic types of avalanches.

Resources

Books

Bishop, Amanda. *Avalanche and Landslide Alert!* New York: Crabtree Publishing Company, 2005.

Merrick, Patrick. *Avalanches*. Mankato, MN: The Child's World, 2015.

Important Words

asphyxiation (as-fik-see-AY-shun) — death from a lack of breathable air

beacon (BEE-kuhn) — a radio transmitter carried by skiers and others that sends out signals to help rescuers find them if they're lost in an avalanche

debris (duh-BREE) — the pieces of something that has been broken or destroyed

glacier (GLAY-shur) — a slow-moving mass of ice found in mountain valleys or polar regions

incline (IN-kline) — a slanted slope or surface

probes (PROHBZ) — thin, long rods used to locate avalanche victims under the snow

snowpacks (SNO-paks) — the accumulated winter snowfall in a mountain region

Index

Page numbers in **bold** indicate illustrations.

About the Author

Steven Otfinoski has written more than 170 books for young readers. He has written books about blizzards, volcanoes, and other natural disasters. He also teaches writing at two universities in Connecticut, where he lives with his family.